GAUDÍ

Photographs: Mike Merchant, Luis Miguel Ramos Blanco, Tavisa, Miquel Badia, Toni Ancillo and FISA-Escudo de Oro Photographic Archives.

Text, design, lay-out and printing completely created
by the technical department of
EDITORIAL FISA ESCUDO DE ORO S.A.

⊽ ESCUDO DE ORO

Antoni Gaudí in the Corpus Christi procession in 1924 (flight of stairs of the cathedral in Barcelona), and President Prat de la Riba and Bishop Reig on a visit to Sagrada Familia, listening to Gaudí giving explanations.

INTRODUCTION

Antoni Gaudí i Cornet was born on the 25th of June 1852 in Reus although there is speculation about the possibility that he might have been born in Riudoms, a village situated only 4 kilometres away where his parents owned a small house. He was the fifth and last child of Francesc Gaudí i Serra, a boilermaker, and Antònia Cornet i Bertran who also came from a family of boilermakers. This fact was to prove a determining factor in the professional trajectory of Gaudí. It was he himself who said, in his old age, that his sense of space became apparent to him in his father's workshop and with the copper tubes that his father handled. As regard his brothers and sisters, two of them died at a very early age, one at the age of two the other at the age of four. Another of his brothers, Francesc, died for reasons unknown in 1876 shortly after graduating with a degree in Medicine. His death was shortly followed by that of their mother and later his elder sister, Rosa, in 1879, leaving to Gaudí the charge of her little daughter. The little girl and Gaudí's father moved with him to Barcelona. Gaudí's father passed away in 1906 at the age of 93 and his niece an infirm woman who never enjoyed good heath, died in 1912 at the age of 36.

Antoni Gaudí did not enjoy a strong healthy constitution either. As a child he was diagnosed as having rheumatic problems which prevented him from playing with other children although he did go out for long walks, a custom which he continued up until the end of his life. This immobility which he often suffered from sharpened a sense of observation in the young Gaudí leading him to discover, with great fascination, the great spectacle offered by Nature. This was his principal source of inspiration for decorating all of his works and provided him with the solution to many problems that his construction projects posed. In fact his method of working was inspired by Nature, a process

Antoni Gaudí in 1878. Original photograph, one of the few existing portraits of Gaudí, exhibited in the Museum of Reus.

Facade giving on to the garden of the cooperative social club «La Obrera Mataronense», project carried out in 1878. (Source: E. Casanelles).

that has come to be known as «organic construction» by which one idea is adds to another and transforms as it grows.

Another important aspect of his childhood noted by many writers, is the fact that he came from the village of Reus, and by association, from the countryside of Tarragona. Tenacity, stubbornness, and strong willed, are characteristic traits associated with the people of Reus and were traits observed in Gaudí himself. It was his tenacity and stubbornness that allowed Gaudí to carry on with his vanguard projects and ideas in the face of opposition. This was even more the case when the greater part of the society in which he lived, including critics and more than one of his clients, did not view positively all that he was trying to do.

Gaudí did not figure as a brilliant student. But, he was an excellent draughtsman and much of his university work already demonstrated his unusual creativity. The greater part of his preoccupation about art was stimulated by books and his own experience. From the outset of his university career he worked in the offices of various architects as much to learn his profession as to pay his way through university.

At the same time Gaudí took part in various «tertulias» (café society discussion

Entrance of the Bodegues Güell, a work of F. Berenguer i Mestres (1895-1897) to which Gaudí very likely collaborated. His influence can be seen above all in the parabolic arches and in the roof conception. The iron door of the entrance also presents the same disposition as the Güell Pavilions.

gatherings) which had strong Catalan and even anticlerical tendencies, although the latter contrasts with Gaudí's progressively growing religious beliefs as time passed. Similarly, Gaudí came into contact with workers movements and the concept of cooperative worker efforts of the period. In fact, his first major job was a project for a factory and a workers quarter for the Workers' Cooperative Society of Mataró (1878-1882). Unfortunately the initiative of this Cooperative Society failed and resulted in only two houses being built.

The city of Mataró also left its mark on Gaudí at a personal level. It was here that the only documented romantic episode related to Gaudí took place. It seems that the affair did not prosper as the girl in question decided in favour of another suitor. And so Gaudí remained a bachelor for the rest of his life, and although the reasons are unknown what is clear is that he buried himself in architecture and his work with a sense of complete dedication.

1878 was a key year in the professional life of Gaudí, it was then that he was awarded the title of architect. He carried out the aforementioned project for the Obrera Mataronense. The Ajuntament of Barcelona (Local Government)

In 1900 Gaudí accepted the assignment for the Spiritual League of Our Lady of Montserrat to carry out the first of fifteen groups of sculptures corresponding to the «rosary mystery» in the route that goes from the monastery to Santa Cova. However, the idea for the figure of Christ did not meet with approval and for this reason Gaudí abandoned the project. It was finished by J. Llimona.

charged him with the responsibility of designing a street lamp for the Plaça Reial, and Manuel Vicens put him in charge of what would be his first house. But, most important of all, he met Eusebi Güell i Bacigalupi (1846-1918) who was his main defender and patron.

This rich industrialist had seen a very original glass cabinet designed by the young architect Gaudí in Esteve Comella's glove shop and he was fascinated by the cabinet. He wanted to meet Gaudí and invited him to his house. This was the beginning of a deep friendship and mutual admiration between Güell and Gaudí that continued until Güell's death. It was this friendship that made possible the creation of some of the works of genius such as the Pavilions Güell, Güell Palace, Park Güell and the Güell Colony crypt. Likewise, Gaudí carried out a project for Güell in 1883, a hunting pavilion in the Garraf region near Sitges, and it is almost certain that he collaborated in the construction of the Bodegues Güell (also in Garraf).

Prior to his first assignment for Güell, Gaudí carried out two interesting constructions, the Casa Vicens and El Capricho. These were works in which a certain historicist style still predominates with an unequivocal influence of Arabic art but, these already bore the personal Gaudí seal. Moreover, in March 1883 Gaudí was given the charge of architect for the Sagrada Familia Temple. He dedicated practically his entire life to this great work of construction, in fact the last twelve years of his life, from 1914 to 1926, he dedicated his time exclusively to this.

Whilst in the midst of the construction of Güell Palace (1886-1890), Gaudí accepted two new projects: the Episcopal Palace in Astorga and the St. Teresa of Avila College. Moreover during the same period we can add another project, the Casa de los Botines (1891-1892). In 1898 he drew up the first sketches for the Güell Colony church although the work did not begin until 1908. Dur-

Entrance porch to Miralles Estate (1901) in Barcelona where a statue had been installed evoking the architect.

ing the same year, 1898, he undertook the construction of the Casa Calvet.

Later in 1900 he designed the First Mystery of the Glory for the Monastery of Montserrat. He later abandoned the project due to a strong disagreement with the governing board, and began the so-called Torre Bellesguard.

His last works, very personal or Gaudian in style, were the Park Güell (1900-1914), the renovation of the Casa Batlló (1905-1907), the Casa Milà «La Pedrera» (1906-1910), the Güell Colony Crypt (1908-1915) and the Sagrada Familia Temple and its parochial schools. Although the restoration of the Majorca Cathedral (1903-1914), which he later abandoned, must not be forgotten; his participation in the Finca Miralles (1901), where he realised the entrance portico and part of a wall; or the sketches he drew for the construction of a hotel in New York (1908). In the middle of the afternoon on the 7th of June 1926, Gaudí was taking his usual afternoon stroll to the San Felipe Neri church, and as usual caught up in his own thoughts when he was suddenly run over by a tram. He died three days later. He was buried in the Sagrada Familia Temple, the church he loved so much.

Cascade, Ciutadella Park.

CIUTADELLA PARK CASCADE

(1875-1881). Parc de la Ciutadella, Barcelona.

Although strictly speaking this is not one of Gaudí's works it should be valued among the first projects he participated in. At that time, during the decade of the 1870's, Antoni Gaudí, a young student of architecture, found himself working in the offices of several architects to pay for his classes. One of these architects was Josep Fontseré i Mestres, who in 1873 had won the municipal competition for the development project of this park. Among the different constructions pro-jected was the great waterfall next to the artificial lake.

The neoclassic conception of this monument contrasts with the naturalism with which various decorative elements were resolved and it is precisely here where one can attribute the direct influence of Gaudí, at least in their design. One can suppose an extensive collaboration of the young Gaudí in the remaining works by Fontseré in his park development project such as entrance gates and iron-work and the so-called Building of Waters with a large lake in the terrace roof to supply water to the entire enclosure.

THE PLAÇA REIAL STREET LAMPS

(1878-1879). Plaça Reial, Barcelona.

During the period when Barcelona was going through a deep urban transformation following the demolition, in 1854, of the city walls, and there were discussions about how the urbanisation of the Ensanche should be, the configuration of the Plaça Reial took place. This plaza was constructed between 1850 and 1860 over the old land of the Capuchin Convent which had been handed over to the city. Francesc Daniel Mora was the architect who won the competition for this project. The landscaping of this elegant and spacious frame structure was not definitively drawn up until 1878 which was the year that the Local Government charged Gaudí with the task of designing a street lamp to illuminate this space.

Of the two plans presented the one that was carried out was one consisting of two street lamps each with six arms that open out like the branches of a tree. Despite being so young, Gaudí demonstrated a mastery of the materials used in this small project (the constructive rationality is a constant theme in all of his work) by integrating the ornamental elements into the actual construction.

Street lamp, Plaça Reial.

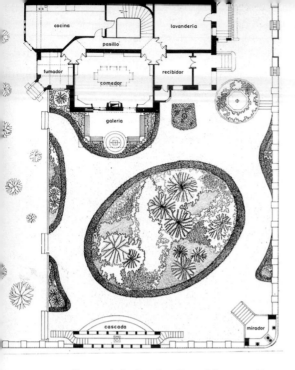

General design for Casa Vicens with a plan of the lower floor according to Gaudí's plan (Source: Bergós).

Casa Vicens from the garden, as constructed by Gaudí (Source: A.H.U.A.D.).

CASA VICENS (1878-1885).
Carrer de les Carolines 18-24,
Barcelona.
Privately owned residence.

In this, the first of Gaudí's grand projects, he already revealed his peculiar genius as an architect and his extravagant sense of fantasy as an artist. The house looks as if it has been taken straight from a fairytale and, bearing this in mind, we have to imagine what the garden would have looked like in its original format as it was significantly modified during extensive alterations carried out in 1925. Also, we need to take into account the widening of the Carrer de les Carolines and the sale of the greater part of this in 1946 and 1962 when two neighbouring houses were erected.

Casa Vicens was built between 1883 and 1885, although Gaudí drew up the plans for it in 1878, the same year he was awarded the title of architect. The young architect was hired by Manuel Vicens, who manufactured bricks and ceramic tiles, to design a summer residence. So, this represents the artist's first important job and in particular his first house project.

The ground plan of the house is essentially rectangular whose form is broken by the advance towards the dining room garden and by the lesser dimen-

Casa Vicens today seen from Carrer de les Carolines. ▷

Detail of a window grille next to the main entrance.

Detail of the entrance gate, imitating palm leaves.

sions of the so-called smoking room. Nevertheless, Gaudí managed to bestow this simple ground plan with a complex titration thanks to the rich conception of the facades. This facade abounds with projections be they small towers or balconies. In order to achieve this, he used stone as the base element combined with bricks and the entire piece is covered with multiple coloured ceramic tiles which were materials closely associated with the building's owner.

As regards the ornamentation and the architectural aspect of the house, Gaudí was principally inspired by the Mude-jar Art. But, one can also catch a glimpse of a constant search for, and application of, new architectural forms and ornamental elements. Furthermore, his concept of architectural works as a whole where one cannot overlook any detail was already patently obvious in his first project. It was the very same Gaudí who designed the original iron railings for the entrance, the windows, of the exquisite and profuse decoration of the dining room, and the smoking room. In short, each corner leaves one with a sense of his strong personality and at the same time creates a clearly different ambience in each space.

Dining room detail, decorated with ornamental motifs inspired in nature.

Door for going out into the garden from the smoking room whose ceiling is decorated with a concave ardornment.

Roof detail of the garden gallery.

Western and southern façade.

General view of the entrance to ▷
«El Capricho».

EL CAPRICHO (1883-1885).
Comillas (Cantabria).
Privately owned residence, since 1988 the location of a restaurant.

As was the case for Casa Vicens, the reminiscences of Arabic Art are striking in this small palace. Gaudí returned to using ceramic tiles as a decorative element although his theme, a sunflower, is more indigenous to the region. Here, one is also reminded of Arabic Art with the slender tower in the form of a minaret which rises up the portico of the main entrance and which bestows the entire piece with a great elegance. It was conceived as a summerhouse for a wealthy bachelor such as was Máximo Díaz de Quijano. Gaudí paid special attention to the lounge, a space for social interaction. Distributed around this principal room are the antechamber, the dining room and the bedrooms for guests whilst the kitchen and the servants bedrooms are located in the ground floor and semi-basement. Finally, the third level of the building is where the attic is situated. Other outstanding elements are the large sash windows that, when operated, emit musical notes, and the work of forging the balustrades of some of the small balconies with metallic tubes that also give off sounds when the windows are opened or closed.

Aerial view of the Güell Pavilions.

THE FINCA GÜELL PAVILIONS

(1884-1887). Avinguda de Pedralbes 7, Barcelona.
Since 1977, the headquarters of the Gaudí Chair.

The first task that Eusebi Güell hired Gaudí for, a hunting pavilion in the lands that he owned in the municipality of Garraf near Sitges, was a project that never went beyond paper. This was 1883. That same year, however, Güell charged him with a new assignment. The Güell summerhouse which was in Les Corts de Sarrià, at that time in the outskirts of Barcelona, had just been extended as a result of the purchase of adjoining lands and Güell wanted Gaudí to design a wall that would embrace the entire property. This wall was to provide three entrances, one main entrance and two secondary, in addition to some alterations to the house itself and other elements of the garden. The old main entrance to the Güell Estate is the work that was so original that we can still contemplate today and which includes the celebrated Dragon Gate. To the left is the porter's lodge, and to the right the stables and the riding school. The rest of the estate was significantly altered after the death of Güell.

On the one hand the opening of the Avinguda Diagonal in 1919 divided this extensive property. The house and part of the gardens were a gift to the Spanish Royal family, transforming the house, between 1919 and 1924 in what today is the Royal Palace of Pedralbes. On the other hand, in 1950 the Universitat de Barcelona acquired various terrains to build the new University City. These terrains included the pavilions at the entrance to the Güell Estate which in 1977 sheltered the Gaudí Chair a branch of the Escola Tècnica Superior d'Arquitectura de Barcelona de la Universitat Politècnica de Catalunya. The other two entrances to the estate designed by Gaudí were much simpler. Having now lost their practical purpose, they were demolished, although one of them was rebuilt in 1953 and today one can contemplate it close by Pharmacy Faculty.

There is no doubt that the most outstanding and eye-catching aspect of the Güell Pavilions is the large door with its notable dragon. This was made from wrought iron, measures

The famous winged dragon at the entrance to the Güell Estate.

The stables after alterations (1977), this space today is used for the library reading room of the Gaudí Chair.

five metres in length and is supported on one side by a brick column that reaches ten metres in height. The expressive nature of the dragon is such that is seems as if the door had been designed solely to create this dragon spectacle. Its aggressive demeanour fulfils perfectly its mission of a creature that jealously guards the extensive estate that opens up behind it. The symbolic value of this creature is transmitted to the Garden of the Hesperides and can be identified with the dragon Ladon that was chained by Hercules. To this symbolic order we must also include the oranges at the pinnacle of the column that supports the door and the position of the dragon's body which is the same as the stars that make up the Dragon and Hercules constellations. The figure of the dragon was one of Gaudí's favourite themes although no other work quite captures the monumental nature of the one here.

The question of the building of the two pavilions that finish off the entire work was resolved by Gaudí with great economy of means as one can see by looking at the materials used. This emphasises once again Gaudí's dedication to details regarding construction and ornamentation even though such details may seem insignificant.

The exterior decoration, which combines coloured ceramics, brick and a set of relief work on the walls, still leave one with a sense of a certain influence from Arab Art, although here Gaudí left his most personal mark in relation to the two earlier works, the Casa Vicens and El Capricho.

In contrast to the profuse exterior decoration the interior of the stables, the riding school and the porter's lodge all make up clean and very functional spaces. The porter's lodge has three bodies, the principal one with an octagonal ground plan with a lowered dome. The stable building is a prolonged construction solely defined by a succession of arches with parabolic outlines.

The riding school, a pavilion next to the stables, is fashioned in a circular form with an upper gallery and a dome which lets in natural light.

These buildings, the porter's lodge, the stables and the riding school, are separated by the entrance door, or the Dragon, although they are stylistically united by their exterior decoration and the small towers which they all end in.

The construction of the Güell Pavilions took place at the same time as the Güell Palace, the work beginning in 1886. However, both construction works represent quite different architectural worlds as do the purposes of each one.

One of the towers of the porter's lodge.

Dome of the riding school.

Entry gates to the palace.

Güell Palace main facade. ▷

GÜELL PALACE (1885-1890)

Carrer Nou de la Rambla 3-5, Barcelona. The headquarter of the «Amics de Güell» Association.

This is a site measuring 18 by 22 metres, a somewhat limited space for erecting what was to be a grand palace for the Güell family. It was to be their city dwelling where they would celebrate their many social gatherings and cultural soirées. Gaudí planned out a magnificent construction from a spatial point of view creating a very complex space in the interior, which gives us the impression of finding ourselves in a much larger palace. The secret lies in the grand salon on the first floor, laid out as an interior patio culminating with an original dome. This main room is of an extraordinary decorative wealth, as in the rest of the rooms and the terrace roof, which has been designed as an equal part of the building. The facade is defined by the first floor gallery and two enormous parabolic arched doors. They were conceived on a large scale to allow carriages to enter as far as the basement where the stables are located. Both doors are decorated with iron grilles upon which the initials of the owner are drawn in the upper part. Between the doors there is an artistic window, corresponding to the porter's lodge, finished off with a kind

Palace basements, in old designated to be the stables.

Vestibule dome, of the first floor large room perforated with multiple circular holes.

of column that is also made of wrought iron where one can see the emblem of Catalonia inscribed.

In 1984, along with Park Güell and the Casa Milà, the Güell Palace was declared part of the Heritage to Humanity by UNESCO.

The terrace of the palace makes up a beautiful garden of sculptures. The centre tower is the finishing touch of the main room dome and the rest are chimneys and ventilation channels. Each of them has a different shape and the majority are covered with coloured tiles.

Main facade of the St. Teresa of Avila College.

ST. TERESA OF AVILA COLLEGE

(1888-1889). Carrer Ganduxer 95-105, Barcelona. Private College.

In 1888, Father Enric d'Ossa i Cervelló, founder of the Society of Santa Teresa de Jesús and dedicated to teaching, hired Gaudí to finish off the partially built St. Teresa of Avila College. The previous architect abandoned the project after only building the first floor. The challenge for Gaudi was to adapt to the reduced budget of the order, and to respect the ideals of poverty and austerity it professed. All together this obliged Gaudí to abstain from all kind of baroque ornamentation and bind himself to the demands of austerity set out by the owner and the purpose of the building as a learning centre. It is precisely here where our interest lies in the St. Teresa of Avila College as it constitutes a magnificent example of construction rationality, and yet at the same time is a very personal piece, even more so taking into account that the building had already been started by another architect.

On top of the existing 60 meter long rectangular ground floor, Gaudí erected a further three floors. To carry out the construction Gaudí used inexpensive materials, such as brick, and resolved the general question the building's construction on the basis of parabolic arches and reducing the decorative elements almost exclusively to pragmatic construction solutions. Bearing this in mind, what needs to be underlined here are the long passages on the first floor, one the most magical spaces created by Gaudí. These are narrow passages with profound perspectives obtained by a succession of parabolic arches lit by natural light that sifts through from the interior patio and the white of the limestone confers upon them an special radiance. On the principal facade, and to gain a certain presence, Gaudí added a small projecting building, something like an enclosed balcony or bay window and which has the function of a porch in the lower part. This porch is enclosed by a splendid grating and wrought iron door which symbolically represents the iconography of the order of Santa Teresa de Jesús. In the centre of this enclosed balcony is the order's coat of arms which is a motif that can also be found on the upper corners of the building. As a finish to the building, there is an elegant succession of crests and crenellations, and in each of the corners there are pinnacles or small towers that culminate in a cross.

Entrance gate to the College, in the bay window porch, made of wrought iron.

View of the first floor passages, a succession of parabolic arches.

Side facade of the Episcopal Palace de Astorga.

EPISCOPAL PALACE OF ASTORGA (1887-1893)

Astorga, León. The headquarters of the Santiago Trail Museum.

In 1887 Gaudí was given the task of erecting the new headquarters for the diocese of the city of León. The former building had been completely destroyed in a fire. The person who charged Gaudí with this task was the bishop of Astorga, Joan B. Grau i Valle-spinós, a friend of the architect and also from the same home town, Reus. Gaudí happily accepted the assignment and the same year presented his first sketches which enthused the bishop. However, the approval of the project depended on the Academy of Fine Arts of San Fernando (Madrid) that demanded several alterations. Gaudí stood firm against them but the Academy would not give in. After modifying the plans twice, the construction was finally initiated in 1889. But in 1893 Bishop Grau died and the work was paralysed. The top floor and the roof were to be finished. When the construction resumed the discrepancies between Gaudí and the Diocesan Council resulted in the irrevocable resignation of the architect. His successor, Ricardo García Guerreta, constructed a very different roof to the one Gaudí had designed a pyramidal-shaped crown, of the same grey-white colour as the facades, with multiple windows. The construction of the palace concluded in 1915, although it was never used as the headquarters of the diocese. At the beginning of the 1960's decade it was restored and now houses the Camino de Santiago Museum.

The palace stands out for its castle like appearance and the use of white granite from the nearby region of Bierzo as its main building material. Although this palace has often been criticised for the way it contrasts with the roseate of the neighbouring cathedral, this grey-white colour can be identified with the clothing of the bishops and is in harmony with the winter snow that covers the ground in this region.

First floor dining room.

Two details of the Casa de los Botines: St. George and the Dragon, window and grille.

CASA DE LOS BOTINES

(1891-1892). Plaza de San Marcelo, León. Since 1929, the head office of a bank.

In 1891 Gaudí has hired by Simón Fernández and Mariano Andrés, fabric merchants who had their business in Léon. The assignment was to erect a large building in the centre of the city that would meet their commercial needs as well as acting as a living residence and with other flats that they would rent out. Gaudí's proposals were approved at the

end of 1891 and work began immediately. The fact that the company founder was called Joan Homs Botinás caused the building to be popularly known as the Casa de los Botines (the play on his surname rendering «botines» has the meanings of «plunder» or «leggings»!). Gaudí laid out a building that openly faced the four winds. The principal facade faced on to the San Marcelo plaza, and this main facade was presided over by a sculpture of St. George and the Dragon, one of Gaudí's favourite themes. The sculpture was moulded in plaster by Llorenç Matamala and sculpted in León by Cantó. The basement opens on to the street to allow in natural light and the ground floor was assigned as a warehouse for fabrics and for the offices. The first floor was assigned as living quarters for the owners, the second and third floors consisted each of four flats to be rented out, and finally, the attic. The entire building is finished off with a two-sided sloping slate tile roof.

The Casa de los Botines, like the Episcopal Palace in Astorga, is characterised by its sobering structure made of stone in sharp contrast to the colourist architecture practised by Gaudí in Barcelona. The sensation of solidness that the building gives is only broken graceful and elegant towers that rise up from each corner. Likewise, the ornamental aspects are limited to these towers, a sculpture on the principal entrance and windows with a clearly gothic influence.

Casa de los Botines main facade.

General view of the area around the church.

Nativity facade. ▷

SAGRADA FAMILIA BASILICA

(1883-1926). Plaça de la Sagrada Familia, Barcelona.

Gaudí dedicated more than forty years of his life to this great and still unfinished work, in fact he dedicated the last twelve years of his life exclusively to it between the years 1914-1926 declining any other project put before him. He even he moved to live within the precincts of this church. This allowed him to work just as he liked: he could remain as close to the construction work for the maximum amount of time resolve any questions that could come up and discuss the different solutions to be put into effect with the workers.

Although the participation of Gaudí in the temple dates back to 1883 (in 1884 he was appointed director as Francesc de Paula del Villar abandoned the project, leaving the crypt as the only almost completed structure, we decided to introduce this construction project between the two buildings in León and the Casa de Calvet, discussed later. That is to say between 1892 and 1900 when the facade of the Nativity was erect-

Central nave of the crypt and Portico of the Virgin of the Rosary in the cloister.

The Passion Facade and the construction of the naves (May 1999). ▷

ed, although the first of its bell towers (and also the only one that Gaudí saw finished known as Sant Bernabé) was not finished until 1925.

The fact that this church took so long to build was due as much to the actual dimensions of the building as to the resolve of the founders, the Association of Devout Followers of St. Joseph, that this church be solely funded by donations. This last fact meant that work came to a halt on more than one occasion due to the lack of money and it is a well-known anecdote that Gaudí himself helped in fund raising activities on various occasions.

In addition to the Nativity Facade, the sections built by Gaudí include the crypt (completed in 1885), the apse (1891-1895), a part of the cloister, the corresponding portico of the Virgen del Rosario (1899), presenting an original disposition as it surrounds the whole building, and the so-called temple schools (1909-1910), today the administrative offices of the temple, a very simple building but exceptional in its conception and structure.

After Gaudí's death the bell towers of the Nativity facade were finished. A little later, during the Spanish Civil War, the church was the victim of a fire which

Three details of the Porch of Charity: cypress (the Church) where flocks (the faithful) retire, birth of Jesus and angels announcing the Nativity.

resulted in the loss of many drawings and plaster models that Gaudí kept in his workshop. The construction resumed again in 1954 with the western facade or of «the Passion", the iconography of which is about the death of Jesus, designed by Gaudí in 1911 whose sculptures were entrusted to Josep M. Subirachs in 1986. The construction of the naves and vaults started in 1990, following Gaudí's plans, a space, which at present can be enjoyed with its outstanding «tree-shaped» columns. As regards the main facade called La Gloria, dedicated to the resurrection of Christ, Gaudí left structure and volume studies and its iconographic and symbolic plans.

The best work that Gaudí did in the church was the Nativity facade. It is made up of three vestibules which symbolise the three theological virtues: Faith, Hope and Charity, all of them displaying a profusion of sculptures more realist than artistic to illustrate in a didactic manner the various moments in the life of Christ. The exceptional and colossal construction at the Sagrada Familia Temple will conclude when the 18 bell towers Gaudí planned are concluded: four of them between 98 and 112 metres in height, on each one of the facades

Spiral staircase in one of the bell towers.

Interior of a belltower. ▷

representing the 12 apostles, five on top of the transept representing Jesus surrounded by the 4 evangelists, the tower of Jesus rising up to 170 metres, and the last bell tower covering the apse dedicated to the Virgin Mary.

These bell towers emerge from the vestibules and rise up to a height of 100 metres. They are spiral structures, an outward expression of the spiral staircases that wind up along their interiors. In the empty spaces at the highest point of the bell towers, Gaudí foresaw placing tubular bells. This sound would combine with that of the five organs inside the church and with the 1,500 voices of the choir that would extend along both sides of the nave and the wall of the Glory facade. Along the final section of each bell tower you can read «Hosanna Excelsis». Finally, as a finish to the towers there are some geometric figures of colourist notes that symbolise the apostles represented by Episcopal signs: the ring, mitre, crosier and the cross.

Detail of the balcony over the main entrance. The letter «C» identifies the initial of the owner of the building.

Casa Calvet main facade. ▷

CASA CALVET (1898-1900).
Carrer Casp 48, Barcelona.
Privately owned housing.

This is a typical middle class house in the Eixample district of Barcelona that Gaudí designed for the widow of Pere M. Calvet i Carbonell, manufacturer of fabrics. At a structural and construction level it is the most conventional of Gaudí's buildings. For this reason it is significant that it is also the only building for which Gaudí's was awarded a prize. The prize was annually awarded by the Local Government of Barcelona for the best building in the city and was awarded to Gaudí in 1900. On the stylistic level Gaudí is inclined towards the possibilities the baroque style offers, a style he had already tried out in the Nativity facade in the Sagrada Familia. The major interest in Casa Calvet resides particularly in secondary elements that, like all of Gaudí's works, were very carefully studied and designed by the architect himself and carried out by notable artisans. An outstanding feature is the extensive and magnificent furniture Gaudí designed for the office on the ground floor, part of it has been recuperated and can be contemplated in the same space, today the location of a restaurant.

Entrance lobby mirror where the
wooden bench is reflected that was
also designed by Gaudí.

Entry floor: lift and access staircase to
the flats. ▷

Lower floor office sofa and chair, designed by Gaudí in oakwood.

Entrance door.

Casa Bellesguard main facade. ▷

CASA FIGUERAS OR BELLESGUARD (1900-1902).

Carrer Bellesguard 16-20, Barcelona.
Privately owned residence.

This is situated on the slope of Tibidabo, an enclave from which one has a beautiful panoramic view of Barcelona, hence the name Bellesguard which means «beautiful view». It is also the site where the last Catalan monarch, Martí I l'Humà, had his summer residence built. The extinction of this dynasty and other vicissitudes of history, ended with the abandoning and final disappearance of this old palatial residence. The only remaining witnessing relic being part of the battlement wall and the remains of two of the towers. When Maria Sagués, widow of Jaume Figueras, charged Gaudí with the project of building Bellesguard in 1900, Gaudí himself was inspired by the illustrious past of this historical place. The result of his work was this small and elegant house for a single family and whose style evokes the old medieval castles in what is clearly paying homage to the Catalan gothic style. In the construction of this house Gaudí wasted no time in making use of the remains of the old mansion. The rest

Detail of the stain glass window over the main door seen from the inside, made up of an eight-pointed star that continues to the exterior.

of the materials used mainly came from the area around the house thus achieving a high degree of harmony with the surrounding environment. The ground floor plan of the house is practically square measuring 15 metres along each side. This line is only broken by two small feeder spouts, in the entrance zone and the other corresponding to the tower-bay window. Its structure is stepped and rises from the entrance to the tower-bay window. This slender tower culminates in a five pointed cross below which a person-al interpretation of the Catalan flag is inscribed.

The fact that this is a privately owned house means that we cannot appreciate the rooms in the house interior where one discovers a very personal Gaudí touch, which is far removed from gothic style exterior. For example, each room has a different ceiling even when they follow the same structure of arches and vaults. The most interesting of these ceilings is the one in the attic which is considered by experts in architecture as one of the most successful spaces created by Gaudí.

View from the attic and interior patio staircase on the last floor.

View of the interior patio.

Park Güell main stairway.   *The «dragon of Park Güell".* ▷

PARK GÜELL (1900-1914).
Barcelona Municipal Park.

Park Güell began as a private urban planning project assigned to Gaudí by Eusebi Güell along the style of the city gardens that had blossomed in England during that period. It is this link that explains why the park was assigned the name PARK, using the English «K» rather than «C» as in the Catalan «PARC». However, such an ambitious and innovative project did not enjoy the success that was expected as only two of the projected 62 parcels ended up being sold. Despite this, Gaudí was able to finish his work on the park leaving us with a legacy of one of his most suggestive and successful architectural achievements. In 1962 the entire zone was declared an Artistic Monument by the Local Government of Barcelona, in 1969 the Spanish government declared it a National Monument, and in 1984 UNESCO declared it Heritage to Humanity.

During the first phase of construction (1901-1903), this mountain of 15 hectares bought by Güell, was levelled. Subsequently, internal roads for the urbanisation were built, a large central terrace was conceived and the lower rooms of columns, spaces conceived as a large recreational square and market respectively, and a wall of protection for the

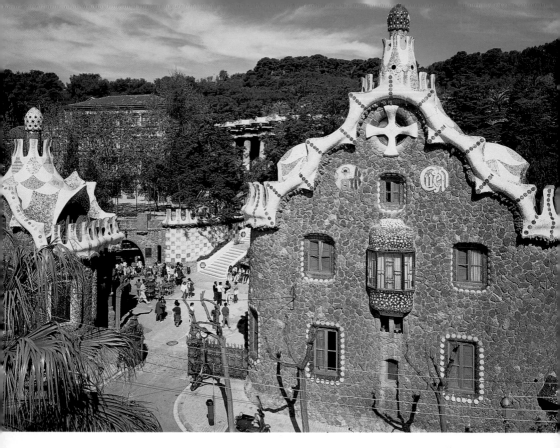

Pavilion destined to be a porter's lodge. The words «Park» and «Güell» are inscribed on its walls.

park was built, the two entrance pavilions (one for the administration and the other for a porter's office) and a model detached house. During the third and last phase (1910-1913) the famous undulated bench was built and the construction of the houses was also planned, but buyers were scarce, because its location was considered too far away from the centre. The only two houses that were constructed date from 1906 and are the works of the architects Juli Batllevell and Francesc Berenguer. Gaudí bought the last one and went to live there. At present it is the Gaudí House Museum. In 1918 the death of Güell completely paralysed the project and his heirs in 1922 offered the park to the Townhall, that converted it into a municipal park.

All features in the Park Güell is admirable and arouse fascination in the visitor: the entrance pavilions, the dragon of the staircase that leads to the Room of Columns, with its original false keystone vaults, the stone viaducts, and in particular the undulated bench of the great central square, for the decoration of which Gaudí relied on the collaboration of the architect Josep M. Jujol (1879-1949), one of his most talented disciples.

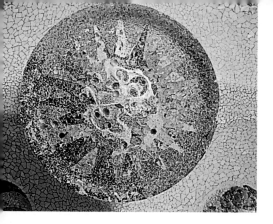
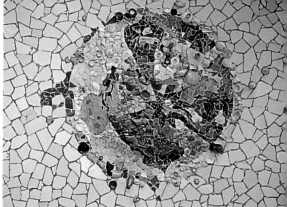

The Room of Columns also called Sala Hipóstila and details of two false vault keystones, extremely original «collages» realised by Josep Maria Jujol.

For the pedestrians pathways Gaudí projected curious arched paths with local stones, looking for forms that imitate the surrounding nature.

Gaudí's House-Museum. Gaudí lived there from 1906 till 1925, when he went to live in the Sagrada Familia Temple.

The undulated bench is one of the major achievements of Park Güell due to its original conception and innovative decoration. This decoration consists of beautiful «collages» made with pieces of ornamental tiles and other very diverse materials.

Episcopal headquarters, in the Royal Chapel, with walls decorated by Gaudí.

Perspective of the main altar with the baldachin created by Gaudí. ▷

MAJORCA CATHEDRAL
(1904-1914). Palma de Mallorca.

The participation of Gaudí in the Cathedral of Palma de Mallorca, at the request of bishop Campins, holder of this diocese, who met the architect on a visit to the Sagrada Familia and was fascinated by his knowledge of ecclesiastic liturgy, consisted of the complete renovation of the temple interior. However, part of the works was unfinished as Gaudí finally gave up the building because of discrepancies with the Cathedral Chapter.

The task of reorganising the interior space basically consisted of: moving the choir from the centre of church to the presbytery, the latter being enlarged; and recovering the large gothic windows and stain glass windows in order to provide the interior with more light. It was precisely the question of illumination that Gaudí studied most. Elsewhere, the main baroque altarpiece was eliminated and the square baldachin of the main altarpiece substituted for one that was octagonal in shape and hung from the ceiling. Other items that were the work of Gaudí and Josep M. Jujol, his main collaborator, were part of the furnishings and decorative elements used on the choir-stalls.

Crowning feature of Casa Batlló.

Main facade. ▷

CASA BATLLÓ (1904-1906).
Passeig de Gràcia 43, Barcelona.
Privately owned residence.

At the same time that Gaudí was working on the Majorca Cathedral and Park Güell, Gaudí was given the assignment of remodelling the house belonging to the Batlló family. This family were another of those wealthy middle class families who operated in the textile industry. Their house was located in the high class district of Gracia just next to the modernist house, Casa Amatller (built between 1898 and 1900 based on the plans by the architect Josep Puig i Cadafalch). The owner, Josep Batlló i Casanovas, had wanted to demolish the already standing building dated 1875 and designed along neoclassical lines and build another. However, Gaudí was against such a decision considering it unnecessary. And so, taking the existing structure as a starting point, Gaudí planned two facades. He completely

redistributed the lower and first floors for which he also designed all the furnishings, and added the basements, fifth floor and interior patio. The end result was this surprising work full of fantasy.

One of the most eye-catching aspects of Casa Batlló is the almost complete lack of straight lines. Concerning the symbolism of the facade there are various interpretations. For some it is a poetic vision of the sea, for others scenes from Carnival. However, probably the most accurate interpretation is that which likens it all to an immense dragon (one of Gaudí's preferred topics) defeated by St. George, patron saint of Catalonia with its symbolic religious transcendence of good overcoming evil. St. George is represented by the lance-tower finished off with a cross plunged into the «spine» of the dragon, whilst the facade is replete with «scales» depicting the dragon with the skulls and bones of its victims. These shapes appear to be inspired by the columns of the first floor and the balconies.

As in all of Gaudí's work even the smallest of details is worthy of mention. We can underline the interior patio in which Gaudí composed an interesting play on light to create a homogenous lighting. There are the

Crowning of Casa Batlló on the rear facade.

Main floor: entrance hall chimney and a detail of one of the room's ceiling.

Matching armchair from the old dining room (today in the Park Güell Gaudí House-Museum).

ceramics that cover it oscillating between white and a gentle blue becoming more intense as one moves up towards the terrace roof. In this space there is an explosion of colour in the finishings of the chimneys and vent shafts. This same effect is a response to the fact that the window and openings in the interior patio are of different sizes for each floor, larger in the lower floors and smaller in the upper floors.

Another detail worth noting are the furnishings that Gaudí designed for the dining room and first floor, and many other secondary elements very often integrated into the actual architecture and that, as a whole, constitute the best of Gaudí's interior work. However, today only the front part has been preserved of the original owner's flat as the furnishings have now passed into the hands of the Gaudí House-Museum in Park Güell.

View of the facade on the corner of Passeig de Gràcia.

CASA MILÀ «LA PEDRERA»

(1905-1910). Passeig de Gràcia, 92, Barcelona. Privately owned living accommodation. Headquarters of the «Fundació Caixa de Catalunya» and «Espai Gaudí».

Whilst Gaudí was finishing the Casa Batlló he accepted a project from the dealer Pere Milà i Camps to design a completely new building as a house also located on Passeig de Gràcia in Barcelona. As construction was progressing and taking shape, this building was baptised by the people of Barcelona, not without certain disdain, with the nickname «Pedrera» which means «a quarry» in Catalan. Also somewhat ironically it was known as «el avispero» (the wasps' nest) and even «la empanada» (the meat pie). These were reactions to the uncertainty that Gaudí's work awoke in public opinion. In the case of this building, he left them in a state of bewilderment as they had never seen anything like it. Many interpret the Casa Milà as a mountain crowned by a great cloud, for others the shapes of its facade were a clear evocation of the rolling sea. There is no doubt that Gaudí took nature as a model and source of inspiration, but it is more than this. It shows the determined will to naturalise architecture, a reverse process to the work done in Park Güell where he architecturalises nature.

Gaudí's initial project included crowning the building with an enormous sculptural ensemble dedicated to the Virgin with the Child, but the owner did not like the image, so in the end it was rejected. But, the inscription to Mary «Ave gratia M plena Dominus tecum» was kept along the entire facade in the undulating line that separates the six habitable floors from the two that make up the lofts.

The entire Casa Milà site covers 1,620 m² joining two buildings, each one organised around a central patio of curved line shapes. Each one has its own entrance: one on the Passeig de Gràcia and the other opening out on to the street Provença. The entire facade was built with large stone slabs taken from the Garraf and Vilafranca areas and each one cut and placed on site. For the decoration of the railings, all of them different, Gaudí relied on the collaboration of Josep Mª Jujol who composed authentic filigrees in wrought iron. The door grilles, designed by Gaudí have quite different lines.

The originality of Casa Milà continues on into the interior, with such innovative elements such as an spiral access ramp leading to the basement for the cars and carriages. Or there is the suppression of the habitual commu-

Balcony with bars sculpted by Josep M. Jujol.

Door to Carrer Provença with grilles drawn by Gaudí.

Upper part of the patio and terrace roof.

nal staircase typical. Instead, Gaudí put forward the idea of allowing access to the floors only by lift or service staircase. Likewise, another feature that needs to be pointed out with respect to the interior organisation of the building is that the entire house is supported on columns and a metal framework with no load bearing walls. This allows the space in each flat to be modified for any purpose.

But, the space that awakens the greatest admiration is the terrace roof. It is made up of a collection of skylights with sinuous shapes, over which the terrace roof runs, and the stepped floor populated with unusual sculptures. These original sculptures correspond with the exits of the service staircases (those of major volume), with the breathing spaces (replete with holes) and with chimneys (which, in-groups take the appearance of severe hooded guardians).

The Casa Milà was declared an Historic-Artistic Monument by the Spanish State in 1969 and Heritage to Humanity by UNESCO in 1984. In 1986 it was restored by the Fundació de la Caixa de Catalunya who have their headquarters here, fitting out the first floor as an exhibition gallery and the skylights in a space dedicated to the work of Gaudí, the «Espai Gaudí». Since 1999 you can visit the flats in the building which are decorated according to the tastes of the period when the building was built.

In the Pedrera terrace roof Gaudí created on the those surprising spaces of all of his works. ▷

Interior of the crypt.

GÜELL COLONY CRYPT (1895-1915). Santa Coloma de Cervelló, Barcelona region.

In 1890, Eusebi Güell, owner of some thirty hectares in Santa Coloma de Cerelló, a town close by Barcelona, founded a large textile complex that included, in addition to the factory and workers' houses, various other items such as gardens, a theatre, cooperatives and a church. But the church soon proved to be too small and so Güell asked Gaudí to build a new church. Although this assignment was negotiated in 1898, the construction work did not begin until 1908 and came to a early halt in 1915. Although the construction remained unfinished (only the crypt and the entrance «portico» were erected) the church was consecrated in 1915.

To understand how Gaudí conceived this church, several of his drawings and sketches have been preserved to give a general idea of the aspect it should have had. He also made a scale model to calculate the balancing forces of the building based on strings from which small sacks with a weight proportional to the pressure that each point had to support. Using this system he was able to obtain a mechanical structure of the building that, seen inverted, demonstrates the resulting spatial effect.

However, the fact that this was an unfinished construction project does not take away the interest the crypt has to offer, in itself it constitutes a masterpiece. As in the case of Park Güell, Gaudí architecturises nature establishing a close and harmonious link between the building and its environment. This link with nature is expressed in the adaptation of the crypt floor to the hill on which it rests, in the materials used, in the organisation of the columns of the entrance portico as if it were an extension of the neighbouring pine grove. This can also be seen in each column, being distinct and original the same as trees are in nature, and in the sinuous ribs that are the vaults and roof coverings. Rather than being a work created by a person it really seems that we are entering into a natural grotto, and this peculiarly is not that case because it is not a subterranean building. What helps to give it an effect of darkness is a carefully thought out aesthetics and study of natural light that sifts through very gently via suggested and colourful stain glass windows. Of the interior, what needs to be featured is the bench ensemble, a work combining metal and wood.

Entrance porch to the crypt.

Detail of the windows.

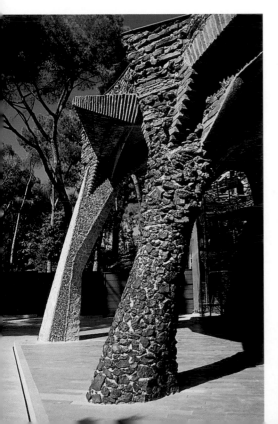

CONTENTS

EDITORIAL FISA ESCUDO DE ORO, S.A.
Tel: 93 230 86 00
www.eoro.com

I.S.B.N. 978-84-378-1632-6
Printed in Spain
Legal Dep. B. 533-2011